GW00492713

Cressida Connolly is a reviewer and journalist who has written for *Vogue*, the *Telegraph*, the *Spectator*, the *Guardian* and numerous other publications. She is the author of four books: *The Happiest Days* (a collection of short stories that won the PEN/Macmillan Silver Pen Award), *The Rare and the Beautiful*, *My Former Heart* and the recent bestseller *After the Party*. She is married to a confetti farmer and lives in Worcestershire.

The
HOOPOE

A MEMOIR IN
FEATHERS AND FOOD

CRESSIDA CONNOLLY

Published by The Cuckoo Press
for John Sandoe (Books) Ltd
10 Blacklands Terrace, London SW3 2SR

A CIP catalogue reference for this book
is available from the British Library

ISBN 978 1 9998219 0 6

Design and cover illustration by Fenella Willis

Printed and bound in the UK by CPI Group (UK) Ltd
Croydon, CR0 4YY

To Anne Dunn

THE HOOPOE

In the baking, rain-starved summer of 1976, I was driven down the length of France and then up again in a rickety Morris Minor Estate. At the wheel was my boyfriend, Bobby: I was sixteen and he was a couple of years older. To say that he was a reckless driver would be a grave understatement. His idea of fun was to fold himself like Meccano into the low-slung car and then drive off at top speed, jumping red lights and storming roundabouts. A 'Give Way' sign was an invitation to charge. He would bellow at the approaches, like a warrior going into battle. I'd shut my eyes and try not to yelp with fear, since screaming only encouraged him. Once he took me and his best friend Sam into the northern suburbs of Newcastle upon Tyne. On Sam's knees (or mine, I forget now which) was a gallon of water in a plastic petrol can. There were two or three more of these on the back seat. The purpose of the trip was to stop people under the pretext of asking directions, then soak them, before madly accelerating away. This was Bobby's notion of a good way to spend a Tuesday evening.

It seems extraordinary to me now that I was allowed on a trip of more than a thousand miles with this near maniac. But of course my mother had never been his passenger. In any case, needs must where the devil drives: my mother had a plan for the summer, which required that I was out of the way. All that spring she had had our family home in Eastbourne on the market. No 'For Sale' sign had been displayed outside: viewings had been arranged to take place during school hours, while I was out of the house. I knew nothing about it. She thought it would be easier like this. Now she had a buyer and, unbeknownst to me, was to pack up the whole house and dispose of half its contents during my time in France. My father had died eighteen months earlier. His library had already gone to The University of Tulsa, Oklahoma.

Bobby was absurdly tall, gangling, impish, with glasses so thick that if you put them on you felt you were lurching through the blurry contours of an acid trip. This I knew because he had introduced me to dropping acid, along with the music of Little Feat and Love, and the gloriously unsophisticated ramblings of the Grateful Dead. We had been on acid, in Brighton, when a friend of his had rolled up on an old Triumph 750 motorbike. That might have been why it seemed like a good idea to take all my clothes off, sit on the back and be roared along the seafront. The arresting officer greeted my nakedness matter-of-factly.

I met Bobby when I was almost fifteen and we spent the next two years together. I had been expelled from my boarding school and now went to a day school, when I got around to it; he had been chucked out of Shrewsbury and dispatched to the south coast to be coached for his A levels. Academia wasn't his thing. I have no memory of him so much as looking at a book, although he would sometimes pore over the album notes and lyric sheets of his record collection. Decades later, I included a comic account of him and his precious records in my first novel. I sent him a copy and told him the page numbers where he'd find himself. It was two pages long, the bit with him in, but he just couldn't. 'Darling,' he protested, 'I can't be expected to read!' What he liked instead was living, doing stuff. Quite soon this became taking stuff.

In the two years we spent together, Bobby was already an avid joint-smoker, acid-dropper and speed-snorter, although I never saw him become twitchy if no drugs were to hand. He once took me to a Chelsea flat occupied by the film-star-handsome son of a famous racing commentator, where for the first time I experienced the glazed remoteness of people on heroin. These were silent young men in pale jeans and dark velvet jackets. They wore scrappy little silk scarves and draped themselves across the arms of chairs. They didn't go in for jokes, or even smiling. The fridge, when opened to reveal the stash of cannabis resin we were there for Bobby to buy, was dismayingly bare. Just dope and the resident light bulb. I felt pity for these poor, blanched young men: whatever did they eat? Out in the street afterwards, Bobby told me – not without a note of approval – that the people we'd just been in the company of were junkies.

At the time I believed Bobby was fine. Nobody ever said otherwise. High spirits, it was called. Nowadays someone might be more alert to the warning signs, but no one was looking. His father was distracted and his mother had gone. She'd run off with a history professor who looked a bit like Jack Nicholson. Bobby's mother wore Indian skirts and beads and her voice was husky with smoke. It was the tail end of the shampoo-and-set era – the headscarf was still ubiquitous, knotted under the chin – but she wore her hair loose and straight, like a child. She had, quite literally, let her hair down. She didn't seem to disapprove of anything.

Her former husband was desolate. He attempted to keep order in the large family home in the North, but it wasn't easy. He didn't have much of a clue. The four children all sided passionately with their beloved dad, but they had their mother's wildness running through them. Their family home, like mine, was a place where someone was missing.

Bobby's father had one leg. At night he unstrapped the artificial one and sat it on a chair in his dressing room, which was next to Bobby's bedroom. He used a crutch to get along the landing. Bobby was in the habit of peeing out of the window – as a bleached patch on the lawn below testified – but when I darted out to the loo in the night I'd see the false leg, sitting on its chair. The leg still wore its sock and polished shoe, the laces neatly tied, while its owner was asleep in his pyjamas. It spooked me and I always hurried past it.

There was a sister among the three brothers, but she was barely ten. I was fifteen by the time of my first visit, so I – being a female – was the only possible candidate to take over at the stove. I rang my mother in Sussex to ask how to make the white sauce for macaroni cheese. This was the favourite of the eight-year-old brother who was coming back from prep school that evening. I had never made a béchamel sauce before. I don't think I'd ever cooked anything, except Findus Cheese Crispy Pancakes and Ready Brek. In domestic science at school we'd once made scones. I managed the macaroni cheese, just. But when it was brought to the table, Bobby's father erupted: where were the potatoes to go with it? The macaroni had to go back into a warm oven while mashed potatoes were prepared. The only thing he cooked himself was grouse, roasted on top of a piece of toast. This delicacy was pre-sented to me as a special treat. The toast was spongy with the decaying blood of the game bird, like a wound dressing. I couldn't bring myself to eat it, nor the mouldering bird.

Somehow or another, word of these mishaps in the kitchen must have reached the ears of our family friend Sonia Orwell. The call came to Bobby's house: Sonia was visiting nearby and would come and take me out for lunch. With hindsight I wonder if she really knew people in that part of the country, or if she was making sure I was all right; but perhaps I flatter myself.

Aunt Sonia was such a close and constant presence in my childhood that I never thought to question her title. Although she was actually my brother's godmother, she treated me with great kindness too, and called us both by our family nicknames. She used to dead-head the roses in our garden, a lit cigarette in one hand, secateurs in the other. Sonia was probably my parents' dearest friend. She had been my father's assistant at the literary magazine *Horizon* during the war, and it was he who had introduced her to George Orwell, whom she later married. At prep school in Eastbourne there had been a group of three: Eric Blair (the future Orwell), Cyril Connolly and Cecil Beaton. The former two went on to be schoolfellows at Eton and remained close.

Unlike some of the women in Cyril's circle, who preferred to have him to themselves, Sonia was expansive by temperament; she became very close to my mother and, in time, to me. She was fair and busty with cornflower-blue eyes and wore her hair puffed up and lacquered, so that in photographs she appears older than her years. She never looks as pretty as she was in real life, her natural animation lost in the forced stillness of the picture. In those days people believed you had to stand with the sun behind you when taking photos, so everyone squinted into the camera. If it weren't for the corrective of the studio portrait, it would seem as if a whole generation had tiny eyes. Sonia was also in the habit of narrowing hers when she was thinking or exhaling smoke, both of which she did a lot. She was extremely bossy about practical arrangements. I enjoyed this in her, but not everyone did.

She was also almost pathologically generous. I was under strict instructions from my parents never to say I liked anything when I was in Sonia's company. Of course it was impossible to obey. I once mentioned a pair of boots I'd spotted in Russell & Bromley, just to see what would happen. She bought them for me.

Sonia generally wore a white – sometimes blue-and-white-striped – shirt with the sleeves rolled up a little, a plain A-line skirt with a slender belt, and a wide gold bracelet. Her laugh, which came often, sounded like the final, slightly screechy gurgle of water running out of an old enamel bath. She was given to dropping French phrases into the flow of her talk. Only now does it occur to me that she may have acquired this habit from reading cookery books. There was also a constant stream of famous names: 'Francis' meant Francis Bacon (who had given her the Hermès handbag she was never without), 'Mary' was Mary McCarthy. Marguerite Duras was an intimate and Sonia translated some of her work into English. Edna O'Brien, beautiful with her curling auburn hair, was a younger friend. The constantly invoked 'Jean' was Jean Rhys, who, impoverished in old age, became one of Sonia's Good Causes. Such luminaries really were her pals, part of a wide international circle. Decades later, when I interviewed Maya Angelou for *The Times*, I discovered she had been another dear friend.

Sonia was snobbish about artists and writers, certainly, and I think considered people in other professions to be wildly inferior. The word 'intellectual' was her highest praise, the thing everyone should aspire to. It can't have escaped her notice on first meeting my boyfriend Bobby that he was not an intellectual. Apart from desultorily reading the novels of Aldous Huxley and D H Lawrence and, for some reason, *The Old Man and the Sea*, I wasn't much of one either. I knew a few long words – 'axiomatic' was a favourite – that I thought made me sound clever, but that was it.

I must have told Sonia that I was expected to cook at Bobby's house. When she appeared, she announced that we were going out to obtain cookery books. I think the father was quite taken with her. I had never seen anyone flirt with Sonia before, but there was twinkling. She took me off to the local market town, where there was a bookshop and a greengrocer. In the latter she bought a large bunch of fresh parsley, in the former a set of paperbacks by Elizabeth David. I have them still, pages yellowed, spines broken. In the 1970s a fresh herb was a rarity outside the sophisticated grocers of London. Presumably herbs were grown in the country-side, but they were stocked only at Christmas, for stuffing. To metropolitan, Francophile Sonia, cooking without herbs was unthinkable. Wine and garlic were standard ingredients, as they were in my mother's cooking. Bobby's father, however, was not keen on foreign food. So although I read the books for the pleasure of their descriptions, I seldom attempted to cook from them. There were no photographs to tempt the novice, only occasional little line drawings by

John Minton, Adrian Daintrey and Juliet Renny. Nevertheless, the books showed me for the first time what a recipe was and gave me some idea as to what was required in order to roast a chicken or make a potato gratin. I can't have been much good at it, even with Elizabeth David to light the way. In due course Bobby's father hired a young woman to do the cooking, to my relief and no doubt everybody else's.

Bobby's uncles, his father's brothers, were dotted about the county. They were all hospitable and lived for shooting. It came as a surprise to me to discover that my convention-rejecting boyfriend was a fine shot on a grouse moor. There were picnic lunches on tartan rugs. It was funny to see Bobby in tweed plus fours and thick shooting socks instead of denim and plimsolls. Not that there was anything very odd about dressing up at the time. This was the hey-day of David Bowie. Once or twice I'd dressed Bobby up in women's clothes and put make-up on him. He made a very pretty girl: actually his looks were better as a girl than as a boy. Apart from his height – he was six foot four – he was quite androgynous, with a smooth chest and not much facial hair. His spectacles made his eyes look tiny, but without them his eyes were wide and round, with a look of permanent amazement, like a cheap doll. He had a wide mouth and one of his front teeth was chipped. He looked harmless.

The uncles had silver pheasants on their dining room tables. For formal Saturday nights the men wore dinner jackets and the women long skirts, even if the company were all close relations. After dinner the women were expected to leave the room, a custom I had never encountered before. I would be taken through to some little sitting room full of floral sofas and spindly tables and told in a lowered voice which upstairs door was the bathroom. Women went up. There was strict segregation in these matters. Men in such houses were expected to use the downstairs loo. Here there was invariably hard loo paper, Bronco. The little rectangles of brittle, waxed paper were always kept in a shallow basket, on top of a pile of old copies of *Punch* or books of cartoons by Giles.

Neighbours with double-barrelled names often gave dances. From time to time Bobby would steal things from the jewellery boxes and camphor-scented wardrobes he found in upper rooms, and give them as presents to me: a necklace strung with amethysts, a mink evening stole.

It never occurred to me to demur. Sometimes he would go off and kiss another girl, or more. That's probably what took him up the stairs to the plundering rooms. He was always penitent afterwards, though not about the stolen items.

With Bobby's father out of the way at the family firm, the days were free for us to do as we liked. We drove around in the maroon Morris. Sometimes we went to swim in an abandoned quarry up in the hills. Once we got hold of some ponies, but Bobby was too daredevil a rider for me and I got frightened when he whipped the rump of my horse, causing it to gallop downhill, shoes slipping on the lane. Often his friend Sam would appear and we'd listen to records. Bowie's *Young Americans* got a lot of play. Mostly we'd loll on the grass, talking. Everything we had to say seemed pretty important. The boys took it in turn to roll joints.

Bobby made people laugh, so no one stayed cross with him for long. All of his stories were at his own expense, tales about his outlandish behaviour and the trouble it got him into. Often the comedy involved him stumbling upon some unlikely object or scenario. 'Funny thing,' he'd say, 'I thought I was getting an early night, watching telly, but when I woke up this morning there were three people in my bed.' The line was always 'funny thing', as if the predicaments he found himself in were not of his own making. He was a master of bluster and indignation, in language he'd copied from his father. It was as if a retired colonel from Tunbridge had taken up residence inside this feckless, long-haired boy.

On the few occasions I saw him in later years, the stories had taken on a darker tinge. The it-was-nothing-to-do-with-me phrasing and delivery remained. He may have been exaggerating when he told me: 'Funny thing, I was just on my way home and next thing I knew it was two days later and I was in a hotel in Mayfair with my brother and two naked Russian women and a carrier bag full of drugs.' By then, drugs always featured in the stories. He had his own shooting parties now. He told me that, after a day firing at pheasants, the mantelpiece in the sitting room would be covered with pills and little packets for the guests to enjoy.

In that summer of 1976 Sonia Orwell saw a great deal of us, for we were all guests at the Provençal home of the artists Anne Dunn and Rodrigo Moynihan. Here the food was just of the kind Elizabeth David described so glowingly: *soupe au pistou, bouillabaisse, salade Niçoise*. Anne, like Sonia and my mother, was an excellent cook. There was a gaggle of teenagers, the friends of the Moynihans' young son. People came and went. A famous American artist arrived, with a beautiful daughter in tow: Bobby was seen canoodling with her. Our hosts were in their studios from early in the mornings until after tea, when they swam. Sonia read and went for long walks by herself. The writer Gavin Young came to visit, having been living among the Marsh Arabs of the Euphrates.

Young believed he'd spotted a hoopoe at the Moynihans' while he was out for an evening stroll. After this, Sonia was overtaken with a desire to see the bird. Late in the afternoons she'd go out walking and searching. Then, as now, a hoopoe was a rare visitor. She thought she might have heard a call, but she never did see one. Rodrigo teased her about it. The daily quest for the hoopoe became a bit of a running joke, the first thing we talked about when we congregated around the huge stone table under the fig tree for drinks before dinner. There was discussion about the representation of such birds in ancient frescoes and paintings. The adults seemed to think that they brought luck.

Sonia hadn't had much luck. At the time I

thought of her as immutable, as all grown-ups were; fixed as a landmark. Luck, or even joy, didn't come into it. But her life had been a catalogue of woes. She was deserted by the great love of her life – her most intellectual intellectual – Maurice Merlaud-Ponty. Orwell died from tuberculosis very soon after they married. (This was not unexpected, but she had been trying to get him to a sanatorium in Switzerland that she'd hoped would help his condition.) A final husband turned out to be gay and rejected her cruelly. In the years after our summer in France together, she became embroiled in a court case with the accountants who handled Orwell's estate, which was to leave her broken and broke. She moved to a tiny room in Paris, then returned to London. There was a frantic quality to her loneliness. She became angry a lot of the time. It was discovered that she had a tumour on her brain, which some thought explained the rage. When I went to visit her at the Brompton Hospital, she insisted I snip and smash every one of the stalks of the flowers I'd brought her, before putting them into water. Bossy to the last. It was only later that I understood that this was an act of kindness, designed to keep me from the shock and sorrow of looking at her too much.

A few days before Bobby and I were due back from the French trip of 1976, my mother telephoned to tell us to go straight from Dover to my sister's house in Kent. Here I learned that the home I'd left a few weeks earlier had been dismantled. She'd gone to Oxford. A year later she married the man she'd moved there to be close to.

After the move to Oxford I broke up with Bobby. At eighteen I went to live in London, bringing Sonia's Elizabeth David books with me. Soon after, a friend brought the man who would later become my second husband round to dinner and for the first time I made *poulet a l'estragon*, from *French Country Cooking*. At twenty-one, I met Adrian (Adrian Anthony, hence AA) Gill. We married in haste, almost as a dare, and took up residence in a basement flat off the Northcote Road. The Elizabeth David books came with us: they were the only cookery books we had. Adrian had a black lurcher, Lily, who I used to take for walks on Wandsworth Common. He was always drawing, a tin of Special Brew at hand, Radio 4 a constant background; we both smoked non-stop and often talked for half the night, only falling asleep as the dawn chorus started. We got a pair of love-birds, as brightly coloured as little flying man-goes. Their cage door was always kept open so they flew about the sitting room, perching on top of the tall overmantel mirror, squawking at the dog. Every now and again they'd shed the odd feather and I'd keep the prettiest ones, tuck-ing them at random between the pages of my books. For years afterwards they would flutter out occasionally when I took an old volume down from a shelf.

At that time it was Adrian's brother Nick who was the foodie of the family. He was chef at Hambleton Hall in Rutland, where he'd earned a Michelin star. When Nick came over he would made a soufflé for us all, miraculously frothing the egg whites with a balloon whisk in a just few seconds. Adrian and I were greedy but not yet accomplished. We cooked most evenings. Together we made terrine, weighing it down with bricks left over from some building work. From *Summer Cooking* I attempted *vitello tonnato* and mackerel with *sauce rémoulade*: both really nasty, never to be tried again. Adrian made a very good beef daube, with orange peel and bay. I made onion tart and veal escalopes with vermouth and cream.

A year and a half later I decamped to Worcestershire, where the man I'd once made the tarragon chicken for lived on a farm. It turned out that he didn't actually much like tarragon. The Elizabeth Davids were installed on the old dresser in his kitchen. That first summer he grew courgettes in the garden and I made Gruyère and courgette soufflés from *French Provincial Cooking*. We got a grey cockatiel and called him Elvis, on account of his jaunty quiff. He had tiny patches of high colour on his pale yellow cheeks, like spots of rouge.

To my surprise and delight, the books Sonia gave me more than forty years ago are still in the same place, and so am I. Nowadays they keep company with lavishly illustrated recipe books like *The Smitten Kitchen Cookbook*, *Persiana* and assorted Ottolenghis. And, of course, Adrian's cookbooks. When the bookshelves had to be repainted last year it gave me a frisson of guilty pleasure to chuck out the novels of Thomas Hardy, paperbacks I'd also acquired in my teens. (I kept Hardy's poems: the gloom is bearable in smaller doses.) But the Elizabeth Davids survived the cull, many of their pages crinkled and stained from decades' worth of spills.

Over time I forgot all about Sonia's obsession, that summer, with the elusive Hoopoe. In the years after we parted, Bobby had an inevitable spell as a heroin addict before the marvellously strong woman he married got him into rehab. Before that there'd been a stint in the army, brought to an abrupt end when he attempted to hold up a bank with a realistic-looking water pistol. We both had children. Every now and again I'd hear snippets about him. The dam of post-rehab sobriety had eventually broken. There were were said to be binges, missing days. Marathon lunches with thousand-pound bottles of wine and outrageous anecdotes. Eventually he didn't seem to have his swanky job in the city any more, or any job.

Then in 2016 David Bowie died, and soon afterwards I got a call. The music of that era reminded Bobby of me: it had been too long, what about lunch? He insisted that we eat at an expensive place in Mayfair. 'There's only one restaurant in London,' he said. It had a lot of carpet. We were there for a good while, during which Bobby drank two bottles of red Burgundy before starting on the brandies. It was really great to see him. We laughed a lot. He said how happy he was at home, how well he and his wife got on. He still loved all the music we'd listened to during our youth and had even made friends, over the internet, with the Alessi Brothers of 'Oh Lori' fame. When I sang a line from that song he looked astonished: 'I didn't know you could sing,' he said. I felt stupidly pleased with myself.

I hardly ever considered the period of my life he'd played such a large part in. There was no one much left to remind me. My teenage self seemed remote, someone I was a bit ashamed of. I wasn't confident that remembering brought happiness, or even much clarity. I'm still not sure, but it was certainly nice to reminisce that day, to feel that I wasn't alone in all the world with this particular set of memories. Are we still the same person throughout our lives? It didn't feel like it, in my case. But Bobby's laugh, the chipped tooth, the pockets of vulnerability and the bluster: he hadn't changed. Seeing him was like reinstating long-lost snapshots in a photograph album.

We agreed that we would meet again, with our spouses too. There was talk of weekends, of seeing each other's mother again, of meeting the grown-up children. Declarations of affection. It was all very cheery and light. But on the pavement, as we hugged goodbye, tears gathered. I heard myself say: 'Oh, Bobby, I feel we may never meet again, in this life.' I don't know why this sense of loss came over me. Just the maths, perhaps. We hadn't seen each other for almost twenty years: if another twenty went by, we'd both be pushing eighty by the next time. Bobby brushed this aside – we'd be seeing each other in a matter of weeks, or anyway months. We were proper friends now.

After that lunch, many long-forgotten memories of the 1970s bubbled up and I looked forward to mulling them over with Bobby. A lot of songs from the time came back into my head: 'Arcadian Driftwood' by The Band, 'Doctor Wu' by Steely Dan, the Grateful Dead's 'Eyes of the World'. A couple of months went by and then, at a party, someone came up and asked if I'd heard about Bobby. There'd been an accident. He was in hospital, unconscious. If he didn't die, it was likely that there'd be massive brain damage.

By the time I went to see him, he was out of danger but still hospitalised. I was told that he couldn't swallow by himself. He couldn't walk or stand. I imagined two scenarios, both vaguely gleaned from TV and film. In the first, he'd be lying prone, eyes shut, machines bleeping around his head. In the second, he'd know me at once. He'd grin in recognition. Put out a hand, perhaps, to be taken in mine. The reality did not didn't resemble either of these scenes. Instead, Bobby was wide awake, propped up in his narrow bed. He didn't look unhappy, that was something. A radio was playing. When I went into the room, he looked up at the sound of my greeting, and then straight through me. I think he knew someone had come into the room, but I might have been a nurse or a cleaner. One hand kept going to the tracheotomy tube at his throat, plucking at it over and over again. He couldn't speak, but insistent noises came out. They may have sounded like words to him. The only thing that was familiar was a gesture. When he forgot for a moment about the tube, his hand went instead to his face, raising two fingers to push his glasses up his nose. He'd always done that. But he wasn't wearing any spectacles. Without them his eyes were round, glassily empty.

Back at home, walking on the green margins of a field by the river, I found a feather. Two or three inches long, black with distinctive white spots. A lovely thing. So pretty that surely it would bring luck. I brought it back to the house, where my husband was excited to think it might be a from a hoopoe. He thought some-one had mentioned seeing one on the farm, the summer before. I put posted a picture of the feather on Instagram and several people said it looked like a hoopoe's. It did.

The feather made me recall Sonia's search. Now I was more or less the same age as she had been in the summer of 1976. I wondered what she had really been looking for in her quest for the hoopoe. Was she just trying to stave off the first drink of the day? Was there some sort of competition with Gavin Young that I was unaware of? Did she truly believe the bird brought luck? How unhappy was she?

A couple of weeks later my younger brother and his wife, both keen birdwatchers, came to dinner. I made roast lamb, but I didn't use a recipe; by then I'd absorbed Elizabeth David's ideas about food and only referred to her books when short of inspiration. After we'd eaten I was excited to show them the spotted feather. It wasn't very likely to be a hoopoe's, they said. Probably it had come from a spotted woodpecker.